Margarethe Bacha

Sweet Temptations

Desserts

Cookery Editor Sonia Allison

Series Editor Wendy Hobson

foulsham

Delicious Desserts

Every chef and every gourmet has his or her own 'designer' label dessert to round off a special menu or meal and there is no reason at all why the home cook should not have a similar repertoire of creative and unusual puddings – temptingly fanciful, visually beautiful and a joy to eat. Hence this book – a superb collection of recipes which are as delicious to eat as they are beautiful to look at.

About the Recipes

1 Do not mix metric, Imperial or American measures. Follow one set only.

2 Spoon measurements are level.

3 Eggs are size 3.

4 Kcals and kJs given are approximate and refer to one portion.

5 Preparation times include both preparation and cooking times and are approximate.

6 Temperatures given are for conventional ovens. Lower temperatures may be sufficient for fan-assisted ovens so consult the manufacturer's handbook.

Contents

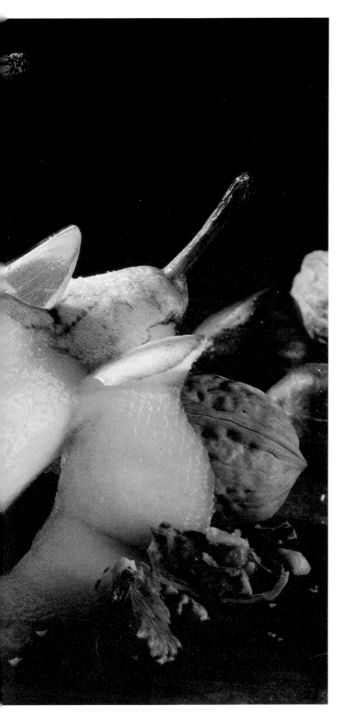

New Ideas for all Occasions

The recipes and ideas in this book cover not only desserts, some of which can double as accompaniments to afternoon tea, but also cocktail savouries such as Stilton Cheese and Cabbage Strudel.

It is Easy to Start

We have brought together a very varied range of recipes in this book.

There are recipes which are very easy to prepare and others which require rather more ability; some are ready in no time at all, others are better planned well in advance.

All the recipes are written so that they are easy to understand and can be followed without difficulty. The flavours used in the basic recipes on pages 15 to 20 can also be varied to suit your own taste. Vanilla can easily be replaced by other flavours (such as cocoa or cinnamon) or other ingredients can be added (such as nuts or fruit.)

However, the secret of success is the same now as in the past, when the home cook spent hour after hour in the kitchen to prepare an impressive and delicious menu. You need the right equipment, best quality ingredients, a good cooker, a pinch of talent and, most important, a little patience. That way, if a recipe does fail the first time, you can succeed the second time – with a little more expertise.

You will need the following equipment and materials to prepare the desserts.

Clingfilm
Use clingfilm to line a water-rinsed mould before a gelatine or other mixture is poured in. This will make it easier to turn out once set and/or frozen. Also the moulded desserts can be lifted out by the film, inverted on to a dish or plate and cut or spooned into suitably-sized portions.

Hair Sieve
A fine mesh sieve is essential for removing very fine residue from fruit purées and some sauces.

Hand-Held Mixer
An electric hand-held mixer is always preferable to a large food mixer because it gives you more control over the consistency of the mixture you are preparing.

Spoons
Wooden spoons are best for dessert cookery because they are more robust than plastic ones.

Kitchen Scales
Choose scales which can

be reset to zero after adding each ingredient. This makes for speed and convenience.

Blender
This piece of equipment is a great help in preparing fruit purées and other mixtures which should be smooth and lump-free.

Fruit Knife
Before you get into trouble preparing fruit with a blunt kitchen knife, you should buy a sharp fruit knife.

Brush
This is used to grease moulds and should have natural, rather than plastic, bristles.

Balloon Whisk
This is a particularly important tool when beating egg whites. As the correct consistency of the beaten whites is vital for some recipes (such as soufflés), the balloon whisk is sometimes better than a hand-held mixer.

Bowls
Metal bowls are best as they neither absorb nor impart flavour and are very good conductors of heat. This saves a great deal of time when beating a mixture over hot water and also when cooling on ice. The bowls should be cauldron shaped, that means they should have a rounded base so that no scraps of ingredients can be left stuck to the bottom edge.

Soufflé Mould
Moulds should have high, straight sides. They can be made from various materials from metal to porcelain.

Forcing Bags
You need a large forcing bag with a star nozzle, for example, for piping cream mixtures on to a plate. A smaller forcing bag with a 00 round nozzle is needed for applying liquid chocolate or for more delicate decorations.

Spatula
This should be made of rubber so that it is flexible; this is the only way to empty a bowl or saucepan cleanly.

Bain Marie
A bain marie or water bath does not have to be a special gadget. It is easier to use a simple stainless steel pan and place an appropriately-sized metal bowl inside it.

Fruit Purées and Sauces

Here are a few recipes which are used frequently in the recipe section which follows and in the plate decorations shown on pages 14 to 15.

Sugar syrup is an important main ingredient in a large number of desserts and is quite simple to make at home. It is often used in the preparation of ice cream and sorbets because its flavour blends quickly and positively with that of the other ingredients. Fruit purées and fruit sauces are also made with sugar syrup.

If the syrup is to be used for a plate decoration, you need to check its consistency before starting, as it should not be too runny. If using fresh fruit in a recipe, always put a handful aside which can later be used for decoration – simple but effective.

Sugar Syrup

Makes 1.5 l/2½ pts/6¼ cups
Preparation time: 5 mins
4000 kcal/16720 kJ

1 l/1¾ pts/4¼ cups water
1 kg/2¼ lb sugar

1 Place the water and sugar in a saucepan and bring to the boil over a moderate heat. Boil for about 5 minutes until the sugar dissolves, brushing down the sides of the pan with a brush to loosen any sugar crystals which have formed.
2 Pour the half-cooked sugar syrup into bottles and seal. The syrup will then keep in the refrigerator for 6 to 8 weeks.
Variation
If you boil 3 vanilla pods in the syrup, this will add a delicious vanilla flavour.

Fruit Sauce

Serves 6
Preparation time: 20 mins
75 kcal/305 kJ

250 g/9 oz ripe fruit (raspberries, bilberries, kiwi fruit, strawberries, pears etc.)
150 ml/¼ pt/⅔ cup Sugar Syrup (page 8)
4 ml/1 tsp gelatine
30 ml/2 tbsp cold water

1 Reserve a few pieces of fruit for decoration and place the remainder with the sugar syrup in a blender. Purée, then sieve into a bowl.
2 Soften gelatine in cold water. Heat 45 ml/3 tbsp fruit purée in a saucepan, add the gelatine and stir over a low heat until dissolved. Stir into the remainder of the fruit purée.
Variation
Instead of using fruit purée, dissolve the gelatine in warmed fruit brandy, wines or fruit liqueurs.

If gelatine is omitted, this produces a delicious fruit sauce. (Essential to omit for kiwi fruits.)

8

Custard Sauce

Serves 6
Preparation time: 30 mins
160 kcal/675 kJ

1 vanilla pod, split

100 ml/3¹/₂ fl oz/6¹/₂ tbsp milk

100 ml/3¹/₂ fl oz/6¹/₂ tbsp single cream

4 egg yolks

50 g/2 oz/¹/₄ cup caster sugar

45 ml/3 tbsp whipping cream, whipped

1 Bring the vanilla pod, milk and cream to the boil.
2 Beat the egg yolks and sugar with a balloon whisk until pale and creamy. Strain the vanilla milk, pour slowly into the egg yolks and return to the pan. Cook over a low heat, stirring continuously, to just below boiling point. The sauce should coat the back of a spoon. If the egg yolks coagulate, place the pan in iced water and beat quickly and thoroughly with a balloon whisk. Allow the sauce to cool.
3 Fold in the whipped cream before serving.

Pear Sauce

Serves 6
Preparation time: 20 mins
105 kcal/430 kJ

350 g/12 oz pears

juice of 1 lemon

250 ml/8 fl oz/1 cup dry white wine

90 ml/6 tbsp Sugar Syrup (page 8)

20 ml/1¹/₂ tbsp pear liqueur (Poires William, for example)

1 Peel the pears, cut into quarters and remove the cores. Sprinkle with the lemon juice.
2 Bring the wine to the boil with the sugar syrup. Add the pears and poach until tender. Purée all the ingredients together in a blender then sieve into a bowl.

Chocolate Sauce

Serves 6
Preparation time: 25 mins
305 kcal/1285 kJ

150 ml/¹/₄ pt/²/₃ cup Sugar Syrup (page 8)

25 g/1 oz/¹/₄ cup cocoa powder

250 ml/8 fl oz/1 cup milk

100 g/4 oz plain chocolate, grated

45 ml/3 tbsp coffee liqueur

40 g/1¹/₂ oz/3 tbsp butter, cut into cubes

1 Bring the sugar syrup to the boil with the cocoa and milk. Add the grated chocolate and bring to the boil again, stirring continuously.
2 Mix in the coffee liqueur and take the saucepan off the heat. If the sauce is too thick, stir in a little warm milk. Finally add the butter and stir until melted. Do not allow the sauce to boil again. Allow to cool before serving.

Preparing a Soufflé

Serves 6
Preparation time: 1¼ hours
215 kcal/900 kJ

The soufflé is the undisputed queen of desserts. Translated from French, the term means a baked pudding, but this simple description does not do justice to the light and foaming delicacy of a classic soufflé. Therefore we shall continue to use the term 'soufflé' for the beaten egg white creations which are as light as a feather, and reserve the word 'pudding' for other cooked desserts with a firmer consistency.

The soufflé has the reputation of being a primadonna: exquisite but difficult to handle. However, if a few basic rules are followed, there is little to go wrong.

The most important ingredient is the beaten egg white which – folded into a flavoured basic mixture – aerates the soufflé and makes it rise.

1 Grease the soufflé moulds with melted butter. Sprinkle first with cake or biscuit crumbs then with sugar. About 25 g/1 oz/2 tbsp is sufficient for 6 moulds. Tip out any surplus crumbs.

2 For 6 portions, bring 200 ml/7 fl oz/scant 1 cup of milk to the boil with the pulp of a vanilla pod.

3 In a second pan, melt 40 g/1½ oz/3 tbsp butter and mix with 50 g/2 oz/½ cup flour. Gradually blend in the hot vanilla milk. Cook, stirring continuously, until the mixture comes to the boil and thickens.

4 Pour the mixture into a bowl and allow to cool slightly. Whisk in 5 egg yolks and continue to whisk until the mixture is very smooth.

5 Place 5 egg whites in a clean and dry bowl. Add a pinch of salt and beat until thick.

7 Fold the egg whites slowly into the basic vanilla mixture. Do this gradually with a whisk, taking care not to overbeat.

9 Transfer the moulds to a baking tray filled with water to come half way up the sides of the moulds, and cook in a preheated oven at 200°C/400°F/gas mark 6 for 30 to 40 minutes. Do not open the oven door at any time while the soufflés are cooking or they will collapse.

6 Gradually beat in 75 g/3 oz/$\frac{1}{3}$ cup caster sugar and continue to beat until the meringue (which it now is) is thick, shiny and stands in stiff peaks when the beaters are lifted out of the bowl.

8 Pour the soufflé into the prepared moulds, making sure that they are only filled to 1 cm/$\frac{1}{2}$ in below the edge.

10 To serve the baked soufflés in the classic way, dust with icing sugar, leave in the mould, place on a plate and wrap each one with a linen table napkin. Serve immediately.

11

Preparing a Parfait

Serves 6
Preparation time: 1¼ hours plus freezing
370 kcal/1540 kJ

Egg yolk, cream and flavouring – nothing else is required for preparing the finest ice cream delicacy known in classic terms as the parfait.

Because of the high proportion of cream it contains, the parfait can be made successfully without an automatic ice cream or sorbet maker.

A parfait which has been frozen in a traditional loaf tin should be decorated with fruit and/or fruit purée.

Do not forget that any flavour is weakened by freezing: the basic mixture should therefore always be flavoured strongly with aromatic ingredients.

Do not leave the parfait in the freezer for too long; up to a maximum of 2 days, otherwise loss of flavour will result. Remove the parfait from the freezer half an hour before serving and leave in the refrigerator before turning out.

1 Rinse a loaf tin with cold water and line generously with clingfilm so that there is a wide border round the top edges. Carefully smooth the film flat.

3 Place the bowl in or over a pan of hot water. Beat the mixture for about 10 minutes with a balloon whisk until it becomes creamy and thick enough to coat the back of a spoon.

2 For 6 portions, place 7 egg yolks in a bowl with 100 ml/3½ fl oz/scant 1 cup vanilla-flavoured sugar syrup (page 8). Stand a damp cloth under the bowl so that it does not slip about when the mixture is stirred. Beat the egg yolks and syrup together with a balloon whisk.

4 If liked, 5 to 10 ml/1 to 2 tsp gelatine can be softened in 30 to 45 ml/2 to 3 tbsp cold water, then heated gently until dissolved. If added to the egg yolks, it will prevent the mixture from separating out.

5 Remove the bowl and place it in iced water. Continue beating the mixture until the mixture is cold.

7 Finish whipping with the balloon whisk so that the thickness of the mixture can be kept under control more effectively. The cream is ready when it is semi-stiff, that means if it is lifted with the balloon whisk, the cream sinks down again gently.

9 Fill the loaf tin, lined with clingfilm, up to 1 cm/$^1/_2$ in below the edge. Smooth the surface and cover with the surplus film. Place in the freezer for 2 to 3 hours.

6 Pour 500 ml/18 fl oz/2$^1/_4$ cups whipping cream into a bowl which has previously been cooled. Whip gently with a hand-held electric mixer until thick.

8 Fold the whipped cream carefully into the vanilla mixture with a large metal tablespoon so that it does not lose volume.

10 Turn the parfait out of the mould or pull it out, using the edges of the film. Cut into slices, dipping the knife into hot water whilst slicing to make sure that the cut edges remain smooth and clean.

Plate Decorations

1 Garnish: Lay 3 semi-circles of Chocolate-Rum Sauce (page 32) 1 cm/$^1/_2$ in apart on a plate. Pour Custard Sauce (page 9) in between.

2 Garnish: Form 3 semi-circles of Raspberry Purée (page 8) 1 cm/$^1/_2$ in apart on a plate. Pour Pear Sauce (page 9) in between.

3 Garnish: Place a small amount of Peppermint Jelly (page 36) on a plate.

Using a knife, draw lines alternately from the inside of the plate to the outside and vice versa.
Serving suggestions: Arrange slices of Orange Parfait alongside, then garnish with orange segments, cream and mint leaves (see pages 30, 31 and 32).

Draw lines 2 cm/$^3/_4$ in apart with a knife from the edge of the plate to the centre.
Serving suggestion: Arrange Cinnamon Parfait alongside and garnish with cream, mint leaves and icing sugar (see pages 34-5).

Cut a fan from the flesh of a mango. Form flowers from 2 strawberries by making criss-cross cuts in each to create 4 petals. Arrange on plate with wine jelly.
Serving suggestion: Place balls of Praline Ice Cream on the plate and garnish with mint leaves and cream (see pages 36-7).

4 Garnish: Put 100 g/4 oz chocolate in a metal bowl and dissolve over hot water. Pour into a small forcing bag with a 00 nozzle and pipe leaf shapes carefully on to a plate.

5 Garnish: Cover the base of a plate with Coffee Sauce (page 56). Apply a circle of softly whipped cream 1 cm/¹/₂ in from the edge.

6 Garnish: Fill the base of a plate with Custard Sauce (page 9). Place dots of Raspberry Purée (page 8) around the edge. Using a sharp knife, draw a circle through the dots along the edge.
Serving suggestion: Turn out a small Raspberry Mould and garnish with fresh raspberries (see pages 60-1).

Fill the leaf shapes with different types of Fruit Purée (here are shown pear, kiwi fruit and raspberry purée; page 8). Serving suggestion: Add Vanilla Cream and garnish with lemon balm (see pages 48-9).

Make curves alternately upwards and downwards using a knife.
Serving Suggestion: Place a slice of Chocolate Mould in the centre of the plate and garnish with mint leaves (see pages 56-7).

Another variation is to use Chocolate Sauce with dots made of Custard Sauce (page 9). Using a knife, draw a circle through the dots around the edge of the plate.
Serving suggestion: Turn out Yoghurt Cream or Vanilla Mould then garnish with cream and lemon balm (see pages 50-1).

15

Soufflés and Puddings

Even someone who does not normally like sweet desserts will be seduced by the delicate taste of an aromatic, light soufflé, by the beguiling aroma of pancakes and cheerfully warm strudel creations from Austria.

Chocolate Soufflé, page 18

Chocolate Soufflé

Serves 6
Preparation time: 50 mins
255 kcal/1065 kJ

| melted butter |
| cake crumbs |
| sugar |
| 150 g/**5 oz** chocolate, grated |
| 25 g/**1 oz**/¹/₄ cup flour |
| 150 ml/¹/₄ **pt**/²/₃ cup milk |
| 4 eggs, separated |
| 75 g/**3 oz**/¹/₃ cup caster sugar |

1 Butter 6 soufflé moulds and sprinkle them with cake crumbs and sugar (see page 10).
2 Mix the chocolate with the flour. Pour the milk into a saucepan and gradually add the chocolate and flour. Cook, stirring continuously, until the mixture boils and thickens.
3 Remove from the heat, stirring, and gradually mix in the egg yolks.
4 Beat the egg whites until stiff, then gradually beat in the sugar. Continue to beat until stiff. Fold carefully into the egg yolk mixture and whip gently until smooth. Transfer to the prepared moulds.
5 Place the moulds in a casserole filled with simmering water (see page 11). Bake in an oven preheated to 200°C/400°F/gas mark 6 for 20 to 25 minutes.

Photograph page 16

Chestnut Soufflé with Coffee Liqueur Zabaglione

Serves 6
Preparation time: 1¹/₄ hours plus soaking and preparation of zabaglione
180 kcal/750 kJ without the Zabaglione

| melted butter |
| cake crumbs |
| sugar |
| 50 g/**2 oz** dried chestnuts, soaked overnight in water |
| salt |
| 25 g/**1 oz**/2 tbsp butter |
| 60 g/**2**¹/₂ **oz**/¹/₄ cup caster sugar |
| 45 ml/**3 tbsp** brandy |
| 6 eggs, separated |
| 1 quantity Coffee Liqueur Zabaglione (page 59) |
| icing sugar to garnish |

1 Butter 6 soufflé moulds and sprinkle with cake crumbs and sugar (see page 10).
2 Drain the chestnuts and remove any brown and stringy bits with a pointed knife. Place the chestnuts in a pan, cover with water, add a little salt and sugar and boil for up to an hour until soft. Drain thoroughly.
3 Heat the butter, add 10 ml/2 tsp sugar and allow it to caramelise. Add the chestnuts and mix well, pour on the brandy and flame. Pass the chestnuts through a sieve. Gradually add the egg yolks, stirring all the time.
4 Slowly beat the egg whites until thick. Gradually beat in the remaining caster sugar and continue beating until stiff. Fold the beaten egg white carefully into the chestnut mixture.
5 Place the mixture into the prepared moulds and bake in a preheated oven at 220°C/425°F/gas mark 7 for 10 to 12 minutes.
6 Arrange the Coffee Liqueur Zabaglione decoratively on 6 plates, turn out the soufflés and place in the centre of the plates. Dust with icing sugar and serve.

Photograph opposite

Gourmet Tip
If you cannot obtain any dried peeled chestnuts, use canned ones. The amount should be about 100 g/4 oz drained weight.

Soufflé with Grand Marnier

Serves 6
Preparation time: 50 mins
320 kcal/1335 kJ

melted butter
*75 g/**3 oz**/³/₄ cup cake crumbs*
sugar
*75 g/**3 oz**/¹/₃ cup butter*
*100 g/**4 oz**/¹/₂ cup caster sugar*
4 eggs, separated
grated rind of 1 orange
*25 g/**1 oz**/¹/₄ cup plain flour*
*25 g/**1 oz**/¹/₄ cup cornflour*
*75 ml/**5 tbsp** Grand Marnier*
icing sugar for dusting

1 Butter 6 soufflé moulds and sprinkle with cake crumbs and sugar (see page 10).
2 Beat the butter with 40 g/1¹/₂ oz/3 tbsp caster sugar until frothy and stir in the egg yolks. Fold in the remaining cake crumbs, orange rind, flour, cornflour and Grand Marnier.
3 Beat the egg whites until thick. Gradually beat in sugar and continue beating until stiff. Fold into the egg yolk mixture, spoon into the moulds and bake for 15 to 20 minutes in a preheated oven at 200°C/400°F/gas mark 6.
4 Dust the soufflés with icing sugar and place each one, still in its mould, in the centre of a plate. Arrange a serviette around it.

Photograph (top)

Curd Cheese Soufflé

Serves 6
Preparation time: 55 mins
190 kcal/795 kJ

melted butter
biscuit crumbs
*175 g/**6 oz** curd cheese*
3 eggs, separated
*75 g/**3 oz**/¹/₃ cup caster sugar*
*40 g/**1¹/₂ oz**/¹/₃ cup ground hazelnuts*
grated rind of 1 lemon
icing sugar to garnish

1 Butter 6 soufflé moulds and sprinkle them with biscuit crumbs and sugar (see page 10).
2 Squeeze out the curd cheese in a cloth. Beat the egg yolks with 25 g/1 oz/2 tbsp caster sugar until frothy. Stir in the curd cheese, nuts and lemon rind.
3 Beat the egg whites until thick. Add the remaining sugar and continue beating until the mixture is very stiff. Fold into the curd cheese mixture then transfer to the moulds. Place in a casserole filled with simmering water (see page 11). Cook in a preheated oven at 200°C/400°F/gas mark 6 for 15 to 20 minutes.
4 Turn out the soufflés on to flat plates and dust with icing sugar. They can be surrounded by Quince Sauce (page 25).

Photograph (bottom)

Apple Soufflé

Serves 6
Preparation time: 1¼ hours
170 kcal/710 kJ

---

melted butter

biscuit crumbs

sugar

250 g/**9 oz** apples, peeled

150 ml/¼ **pt**/²/₃ cup Sugar Syrup (page 8)

juice of ½ lemon

3 eggs, separated

75 g/**3 oz**/¹/₃ cup caster sugar

25 g/**1 oz** fresh root ginger, grated

a pinch of ground cinnamon

icing sugar to garnish

---

1 Butter 6 soufflé moulds and sprinkle with biscuit crumbs and sugar (see page 10).
2 Quarter the apples and remove the cores. Boil with the lemon juice and the sugar syrup until the liquid has evaporated. Purée until smooth in a blender. Beat the egg yolks with 25 g/1 oz/2 tbsp caster sugar until frothy. Carefully fold in the apple purée, ginger and cinnamon.
3 Beat the egg whites until thick. Gradually beat in the rest of the sugar and continue to beat until mixture is very stiff. Carefully fold into the egg yolk mixture and transfer to the moulds. Bake in a preheated oven at 200°C/400°F/gas mark 6 for 25 to 30 minutes.
4 Dust with icing sugar and serve immediately. Do not turn out.

Photograph opposite (top)

Coffee Pudding with Strawberry Sauce

Serves 6
Preparation time: 1½ hours
425 kcal/1774 kJ

---

melted butter

cake crumbs

sugar

75 g/**3 oz**/¹/₃ cup butter

60 g/**2**¹/₂ **oz**/¹/₄ cup caster sugar

25 g/**1 oz**/2 tbsp coffee powder

2 eggs, separated

45 ml/**3 tbsp** coffee liqueur

6 sponge fingers, crumbled

1 quantity Strawberry Purée (page 8)

20 ml/1¹/₂ **tbsp** Grand Marnier

300 ml/¹/₂ **pt**/1 ¹/₄ cups whipped cream

mint leaves

16 strawberries

---

1 Butter 6 soufflé moulds and sprinkle them with cake crumbs and sugar (see page 10).
2 Beat the butter with 40 g/1¹/₂ oz/3 tbsp caster sugar and the coffee powder until fluffy. Add the egg yolks gradually and flavour with the coffee liqueur.
3 Beat the egg whites until thick. Gradually beat in remaining sugar and continue to beat until stiff. Fold into the coffee mixture along with the crumbled sponge fingers. Transfer to moulds and place in a casserole filled with simmering water (see page 11). Bake in a preheated oven at 190°C/375°F/gas mark 5 for 25 to 35 minutes. Flavour the Strawberry Purée with Grand Marnier.
4 Pipe the cream in semi-circles, 1 cm/¹/₂ in apart, on a chilled plate; pour Strawberry Purée in between. Draw a knife across to make patterns as desired.
5 Turn out the pudding and place it attractively on the plate. Garnish with strawberries and mint leaves. If desired, two slices of Nut Parfait (page 36) may also be arranged decoratively on the plate.

Photograph opposite (bottom)

Gourmet Tip
If the pudding browns too quickly on the top, cover it with kitchen foil.

Rice Pudding with Quince Sauce

Serves 6
Preparation time: 2¹/₂ hours
635 kcal/2605 kJ

Sauce:
375 ml/**13 fl oz**/1¹/₂ cups Sugar Syrup (page 8)

75 g/**3 oz** acacia honey

300 ml/¹/₂ pt/1¹/₄ cups white wine

2 cloves

3 large quinces

10 ml/**2 tsp** gelatine

juice of 1 lemon

Pudding:
melted butter

cake crumbs

sugar

500 ml/**18 fl oz**/2¹/₄ cups milk

a pinch of salt

120 g/**5 oz** pudding rice

120 g/**5 oz**/²/₃ cup caster sugar

5 eggs, separated

grated rind of 1 lemon

75 g/**3 oz**/¹/₃ cup butter, cut into flakes

icing sugar to garnish

1 Bring the sugar syrup, honey, wine and cloves to the boil. Allow to boil down for 6 to 8 minutes then remove the cloves. Peel the quinces, cut into quarters and remove the cores. Cut each quarter into thin slices and cook in the sugar syrup until soft.

2 Soften the gelatine in a little cold water. Pour into a pan and melt slowly over a low heat. Stir into the stewed quinces. Season to taste with the lemon juice, put into a bowl and leave in a cool place.

3 Butter 6 soufflé moulds and sprinkle them with cake crumbs and sugar (see page 10).

4 Bring the milk to the boil with the salt, then add the rice, bring back to the boil and cook for about 20 minutes over a lowish heat.

5 Beat 50 g/2 oz/¹/₄ cup caster sugar with the egg yolks until they are frothy. Add the lemon rind and the butter to the rice while it is still warm. Carefully stir in the egg yolk mixture with a wooden spoon and leave in a cool place.

6 Beat the egg whites until they are stiff. Gradually beat in the remaining caster sugar and continue to beat until very stiff. Fold carefully into the cold rice mixture. Put the mixture into the moulds, place in a casserole with simmering water (see page 11) and bake in a preheated oven at 190°C/375°F/gas mark 5 for 30 to 40 minutes.

7 Turn out the puddings on to deep plates, arrange the quince sauce around the puddings, dust with icing sugar and serve immediately.

Walnut and Poppy Seed Pudding

Serves 6
Preparation time: 1¼ hours
490 kcal/2055 kJ

---

melted butter

cake crumbs

75 g/3 oz/¹/₃ cup caster sugar

6 eggs, separated

100 g/4 oz poppy seeds, ground

60 g/2¹/₂ oz/¹/₂ cup walnuts, ground and toasted

50 ml/2 fl oz/¹/₄ cup rum

40 g/1¹/₂ oz/¹/₃ cup cake crumbs

1 quantity Raspberry Purée (page 8)

icing sugar to garnish

---

1 Butter 6 soufflé moulds and sprinkle with crumbs and sugar (page 10).
2 Beat the butter and 50 g/2 oz/¹/₄ cup caster sugar until frothy, then stir in the egg yolks, seeds, walnuts, rum and crumbs.
3 Beat the egg whites until thick. Add the remaining sugar and beat until stiff. Fold into the egg yolks. Put into the moulds, place these in a casserole with simmering water and cook in a preheated oven at 220°C/425°F/gas mark 7 for 20 to 30 minutes.
4 Turn out the puddings and garnish with raspberry purée and icing sugar.

Photograph opposite (top)

Sweet Cabbage Strudel

Serves 6
Preparation time: 2¼ hours plus marinating
305 kcal/1265 kJ

Filling:
10 ml/2 tsp vanilla sugar

20 ml/1¹/₂ tbsp Marc or grappa brandy

50 g/2 oz/¹/₃ cup raisins

600 g/1¹/₄ lb white cabbage (without stalks)

salt

40 g/1¹/₂ oz/3 tbsp butter

Pastry:
100 g/4 oz/1 cup flour

1 egg yolk

20 g/³/₄ oz/1¹/₂ tbsp butter

10 ml/2 tsp vinegar

little lukewarm water

10 ml/2 tsp corn or sunflower oil

---

flour

40 g/1¹/₂ oz/¹/₃ cup walnuts, ground

60 ml/4 tbsp soured cream

melted butter

1 egg yolk

icing sugar to garnish

---

1 Mix the vanilla sugar and the brandy in a basin. Add the raisins and marinate for 3 hours. Cut the cabbage leave into thin strips and salt lightly. Leave to draw for 30 minutes, then squeeze out well. Heat the butter in a pan, add the cabbage and cook gently for about 7 minutes. Add the raisins and mix with the cabbage. Leave to cool.

2 Sieve the flour on to a table and make a well in the centre. Put all the other pastry ingredients into the well and work to a dough by hand. Knead the dough for about 10 to 15 minutes until smooth and form into a ball. Sprinkle some more flour into a bowl, place the dough in the bowl, coat with oil and seal with clingfilm to keep it airtight and prevent it from drying out. Leave the dough to relax for 30 minutes.
3 Place a tea towel on the table and dust with flour. Roll the dough out on this first and then stretch it with your hands until the dough is almost transparent. Sprinkle walnuts on the dough. Cover with the cabbage and raisin mixture then dot with soured cream. Roll up the dough, using the cloth to help. Cut the ends of the dough straight and squeeze together tightly.
4 Place the strudel on a baking tray brushed with melted butter, coat with egg yolk and bake in a preheated oven at 180°C/350°F/gas mark 4 for 20 to 25 minutes. Cut the strudel into slices, place on warmed plates and sprinkle with icing sugar.

Photograph opposite (bottom)

Apricot Dumplings

Serves 6
Preparation time: 2¼ hours
445 kcal/1860 kJ

Dumplings:

600 g/1¼ lb potatoes, washed

40 g/1½ oz/⅓ cup flour

5 egg yolks

salt

a pinch of nutmeg

25 g/1 oz/2 tbsp butter, cut into flakes

45 ml/3 tbsp rum or brandy

18 cubes of sugar

18 apricots

Crumb Coating:

20 g/¾ oz/1½ tbsp caster sugar

25 g/1 oz/2 tbsp butter

40 g/1½ oz/2½ tbsp cake crumbs

1 quantity Fruit Purée (page 8)

1 Wrap the potatoes in kitchen foil and cook in a preheated oven at 220°C/425°F/gas mark 7 for about 1 hour. Scoop out the insides and mix well with the flour, egg yolks, salt, nutmeg and butter.
2 Sprinkle rum or brandy on the sugar. Skin the apricots, carefully cut an incision in each and remove the stones. Place 1 cube of sugar in each. Roll each apricot in a separate piece of potato dough. Cook in simmering salted water for 10 to 15 minutes.
3 Meanwhile, toast the butter, sugar and cake crumbs in a frying pan and allow to cool. Roll the dumplings in the mixture and serve with fruit purée.

Photograph opposite (top)

Pancakes with Wine Cream and Strawberries

Serves 6
Preparation time. 1¼ hours
350 kcal/1465 kJ

Dough:

40 g/1½ oz/⅓ cup flour

25 g/1 oz/¼ cup cornflour

pulp from 1 vanilla pod

4 eggs

a pinch of salt

a pinch of caster sugar

175 ml/6 fl oz/¾ cup single cream

20 g/¾ oz/1½ tbsp butter

extra butter or oil for frying

Wine Cream:

75 g/3 oz/⅓ cup caster sugar

5 egg yolks

juice of 1 lemon

200 ml/7 fl oz/scant 1 cup white wine

225 g/8 oz strawberries, wild if possible

icing sugar to garnish

1 Put the flour, cornflour and vanilla pod pulp in a bowl. Make a well in the centre. Put the eggs, salt and sugar into the well, pour in the cream and beat all the ingredients until smooth. Allow the butter to colour in a pan, then add it to the dough while lukewarm and mix in well.
2 To cook the pancakes, heat a very small amount of butter or oil for each pancake in a heavy pan, then pour enough of the batter into the pan to just cover the base thinly. Fry the pancakes on one side for about 1 minute then turn them over and fry the other side.
3 Immediately you have made each pancake, place it on a large plate in a preheated oven at 110°C/225°F/gas mark ¼. Cover the pancakes with a second plate so that they keep warm and do not dry out.
4 To make the wine cream, mix the sugar, egg yolks and lemon juice together in a bowl then add the white wine. Beat with a balloon whisk over a bowl of hot water until the mixture thickens.
5 Do not wash the strawberries unless you have to, as this causes them to lose flavour.
6 Arrange the pancakes on 6 warmed plates, pour the warm wine cream over them, garnish with the strawberries and sprinkle with icing sugar if desired.

Photograph opposite (bottom)

Frozen
Desserts

Our passion for ice creams and kindred sweets remains constant, and this chapter introduces you to a wonderful world of fantasy ideas for parfaits, ice creams, sorbets and granitas.

Orange Parfait with Chocolate-Rum Sauce, page 32

Orange Parfait with Chocolate-Rum Sauce

Serves 6
Preparation time: 1 hour
plus freezing
940 kcal/3925 kJ

Parfait:

6 egg yolks

2 eggs

200 g/7 oz/scant 1 cup caster sugar

juice and grated rind of 2 oranges

juice of 1 lemon

20 ml/1½ tbsp Cointreau

45 ml/3 tbsp Grand Marnier

150 ml/¼ pt/⅔ cup whipping cream, whipped

150 ml/¼ pt/⅔ cup double cream, whipped

Chocolate-Rum Sauce:

150 ml/¼ pt/⅔ cup Sugar Syrup (page 8)

500 ml/18 fl oz/2¼ cups milk

25 g/1 oz/¼ cup cocoa

120 g/5 oz chocolate, broken into pieces

45 ml/3 tbsp rum

40 g/1½ oz/3 tbsp butter, cut into pieces

1 quantity Custard Sauce (page 9)

12 orange segments

150 ml/¼ pt/⅔ cup whipping cream, whipped

mint leaves

1 To make the parfait, place the egg yolks, eggs and sugar in a bowl and whisk over a pan of hot water until thick. Put the bowl into a larger bowl filled with ice cubes and continue beating until the mixture is cold. Stir in orange rind and juice, the lemon juice and the two liqueurs. Finally fold in the cream and double cream smoothly. Line a loaf tin with clingfilm (see page 12) and fill with the parfait mixture. Leave in the freezer for 4 to 6 hours.
2 Bring the sugar syrup to the boil with the milk and cocoa. Add the chocolate and bring back to the boil, stirring continuously, then pour in the rum. Remove the sauce from the heat and stir in the butter. Do not allow the sauce to boil again. Leave in a cool place.
3 Remove the parfait from the mould and cut into slices. Arrange as shown on page 30, with custard sauce, decorating with orange segments, cream and mint leaves.

Photograph page 30

Ginger Parfait with Pernod

Serves 6
Preparation time: 1 hour
plus freezing
420 kcal/1760 kJ

100 g/4 oz/½ cup caster sugar

10 ml/2 tsp cinnamon

25 g/1 oz marzipan

3 egg yolks

2 eggs

juice and grated rind of 1 orange

40 g/1½ oz ginger biscuits or cake, cubed

40 g/1½ oz ginger biscuits, crumbled

60 ml/4 tbsp Pernod

500 ml/18 fl oz/2¼ cups whipping cream, whipped

1 Place the sugar, cinnamon, marzipan, egg yolks, eggs, orange juice and rind in a bowl and whisk over a saucepan of hot water. Put the bowl into a larger bowl filled with ice cubes and continue beating until the mixture is cold. Fold in the remaining ingredients carefully, reserving 150 ml/¼ pt/⅔ cup whipped cream.
2 Line a loaf tin with clingfilm (see page 12). Fill with the parfait mixture and freeze for 2 to 3 hours.
3 Remove the frozen parfait from the mould, cut into slices and place on chilled plates. Garnish with the reserved whipped cream.

Photograph opposite

33

Mocha Parfait with Orange Liqueur

Serves 6
Preparation time: 1¹/₄ hours plus freezing
565 kcal/2355 kJ

6 egg yolks
2 eggs
200 g/*7 oz*/scant 1 cup caster sugar
50 g/*1¹/₂ oz*/3 tbsp filter coffee powder
300 ml/*¹/₂ pt*/1¹/₄ cups water
8 sponge fingers
45 ml/*3 tbsp* coffee liqueur
45 ml/*3 tbsp* Cointreau
grated rind of 1 orange
500 ml/*1 pint*/2¹/₂ cups double cream, whipped

1 Beat the egg yolks, eggs and sugar. Make the coffee with the water. Stir slowly into the egg mixture and whisk in a bowl over a pan of hot water until thick. Put the bowl into a second bowl full of ice cubes and beat the egg mixture until cold.
2 Line a loaf tin with clingfilm (see page 12). Soak the sponge fingers in half the liqueurs. Fold the remaining liqueurs, orange rind and cream into the egg mixture.
3 Put half the parfait into the mould and freeze for 45 minutes. Place the sponge fingers on top, fill with the remaining parfait and freeze for 3 hours.

Photograph opposite (bottom)

Cinnamon Parfait

Serves 6
Preparation time: 1¼ hours plus freezing
750 kcal/3135 kJ

5 egg yolks
2 eggs
*200 g/**7 oz**/scant 1 cup caster sugar*
*25 g/**1 oz**/2 tbsp cinnamon*
*45 ml/**3 tbsp** rum*
*300 ml/¹/₂ **pt**/²/₃ cup double cream, whipped*
1 quantity Pear Sauce (page 9)
1 quantity Raspberry Purée (page 8)
*150 ml/¹/₄ **pt**/²/₃ cup whipped cream*
mint leaves
icing sugar to garnish

1 Place the egg yolks, eggs, sugar and cinnamon in a bowl and whisk over a pan of hot water until thick. Stand the bowl in a second bowl full of ice cubes and beat until cold. Fold in the rum then the double cream.
2 Line a loaf tin with clingfilm (see page 12) and fill carefully with the parfait mixture. Leave in the freezer for 4 to 6 hours.
3 Take the parfait out of the mould and cut into slices. Use the second garnish from page 14 for decoration (Pear sauce and raspberry purée). Garnish with cream, mint leaves and icing sugar.

Photograph opposite (top)

Nut Parfait

Serves 6
Preparation time: 1¼ hours plus freezing
520 kcal/2670 kJ

---

75 g/*3 oz*/¹/₃ *cup caster sugar*

30 ml/*2 tbsp* honey

25 g/*1 oz* marzipan

3 egg yolks

2 eggs

75 g/*3 oz* ground hazelnuts, roasted under the grill

45 ml/*3 tbsp* cherry brandy or Kirsch

400 ml/*14 fl oz*/1³/₄ cups whipping cream, whipped

1 quantity Fruit Purée (page 8)

---

1 Place the sugar, honey, marzipan, egg yolks and eggs in a bowl and whisk over a pan of hot water until thick. Place the bowl in a larger bowl filled with ice cubes and continue beating the egg mixture until it is cold. Fold in the hazelnuts and the cherry brandy or Kirsch. Finally fold in the cream.
2 Line a loaf tin with clingfilm (see page 12) and fill with the parfait mixture. Freeze for 4 to 6 hours.
3 Remove the parfait from the mould and cut it into slices. Serve with fruit purée.

Photograph opposite (top)

Praline Ice with Mint Jelly and Mango Fans

Serves 6
Preparation time: 1½ hours plus freezing
630 kcal/2635 kJ

Ice Cream:

250 ml/*8 fl oz*/1 cup milk

250 ml/*8 fl oz*/1 cup single cream

30 ml/*2 tbsp* cocoa

75 g/*3 oz* plain chocolate

40 g/1½ *oz* chocolate and hazelnut spread such as Nutella

75 g/*3 oz* cooking chocolate

5 egg yolks

20 g/³/₄ *oz*/1½ tbsp caster sugar

grated rind of 1 orange

20 ml/1½ *tbsp* apricot brandy

20 ml/1½ *tbsp* Cointreau

Jelly:

1 envelope gelatine

30 ml/*2 tbsp* cold water

45 ml/*3 tbsp* mint liqueur

8 sprigs of mint

300 ml/*½ pt*/1¼ cups Sugar Syrup (page 8)

300 ml/*½ pt*/1¼ cups white wine

juice of 2 lemons

---

450 g/*1 lb* mangoes

12 large strawberries

60 ml/*4 tbsp* whipping cream, whipped

---

1 Place the first 6 ingredients in a pan and bring slowly to the boil over a low heat, stirring continu- ously. Beat the egg yolks and sugar to a cream in a bowl. Fold the chocolate mixture carefully into the egg mixture with a balloon whisk, then pass the mix- ture through a fine sieve so that any small lumps of chocolate are removed. Flavour the ice cream mix- ture to taste with the or- ange rind and the alcohol. Allow to cool and freeze in an ice cream or sorbet maker.
2 To make the jelly, soften the gelatine in the cold water, pour into a sauce- pan and melt over a low heat. Stir in the liqueur, heated to lukewarm. Pull the mint leaves away from the stalks (reserve 12 for garnishing). Chop finely and place in a pan. Add the sugar syrup and the wine and boil to reduce the quantity by a third. Stir in the gelatine-liqueur mixture, flavour the mix- ture to taste with lemon juice and leave to cool.
3 Peel the mangoes and remove the flesh from the stones. Arrange the praline ice cream, man- goes and strawberries as shown in the third garnish on page 14. Add the mint leaves and cream to the garnish.

Photograph opposite (bottom)

Walnut Ice Cream with Rhubarb

Serves 6
Preparation time: 2¼ hours plus freezing
600 kcal/2515 kJ

Ice Cream:

150 ml/¹/₄ *pt*/²/₃ *cup milk*

150 ml/¹/₄ *pt*/²/₃ *cup single cream*

2 egg yolks

2 eggs

75 ml/*3 tbsp honey*

75 g/*3 oz*/¹/₃ *cup caster sugar*

20 ml/*1*¹/₂ *tbsp Amaretto*

75 g/*3 oz walnuts, coarsely chopped*

25 g/*1 oz*/2 tbsp sugar

Rhubarb:

450 g/*1 lb rhubarb*

225 g/*8 oz*/1 cup caster sugar

300 ml/¹/₂ *pt*/1 ¹/₄ *cups red wine*

140 ml/¹/₄ *pt*/²/₃ *cup port*

1 stick cinnamon

juice of 1 lemon

1 quantity Cranberry or Raspberry Purée (page 8)

---

1 Bring the milk and cream to the boil in a pan. Beat the egg yolks, eggs, honey and sugar in a second pan until thick and creamy. Fold the boiling milk and cream carefully into the egg mixture; return to the heat briefly and whisk. The mixture must not be allowed to boil. Fold in the Amaretto. Pass the mixture through a sieve and allow to cool. Put the walnuts in a frying pan and roast lightly. Remove from the heat, add the sugar and toss until the mixture has cooled.
2 Freeze the cooled Amaretto mixture in an ice cream or sorbet maker; do not add the roasted nuts until the mixture has a semi-solid consistency. Then complete freezing.
3 Peel the washed rhubarb (red outdoor rhubarb is most suitable). Cut into pieces approximately 4 cm/1¹/₂ in long, sprinkle with about 60 g/2 ¹/₂ oz/¹/₄ cup sugar and allow to draw for at least 30 minutes. Put the remaining sugar and the rest of the ingredients into a pan and boil until the liquid has reduced by three-quarters. Add the rhubarb with the juice and bring to the boil again; add sugar to taste if necessary. Allow to cool.
4 Place three balls of walnut ice cream on each chilled plate and cover with the stewed fruit.

Gourmet Tip
Place the walnut ice cream in chilled soup dishes, cover with the stewed rhubarb and Vanilla Cream (page 48), and brown quickly under a hot grill.

Vanilla Ice with White Peaches

Serves 6
Preparation time: 1¼ hours plus freezing and Curd Cheese Cream preparation
520 kcal/2180 kJ plus curd cheese cream

Ice Cream:

pulp from 1 vanilla pod

300 ml/½ pt/1¼ cups single cream

4 egg yolks

150 g/5 oz/⅔ cup caster sugar

Peaches:

6 white peaches

400 ml/14 fl oz/1¾ cups Sugar Syrup (page 8)

150 ml/¼ pt/⅔ cup white wine

20 ml/1½ tbsp vanilla liqueur or Poires William

5 ml/1 tsp vanilla essence

juice of 1 lemon

1 quantity Curd Cheese Cream (page 51)

1 Bring the vanilla pulp and cream up to the boil in a saucepan. Whip the egg yolks in a second pan with the sugar until thick and creamy. Fold the boiling cream carefully into the egg mixture, heat again briefly and whip. The mixture must not boil. Pass the mixture through a sieve and allow to cool. Freeze in an ice cream or sorbet maker.

2 Scald the peaches with boiling water, peel, then cut in half and remove the stones. Bring the sugar syrup, white wine, vanilla liqueur, vanilla essence and lemon juice to the boil with the peace stones. Add the half peaches and poach to taste. Make sure they are not too soft. Allow the peaches to cool in the liquid.
3 Arrange 2 balls of the vanilla ice cream on chilled oval plates, place half a peach on each ball of ice cream, cover with the curd cream and brown quickly under the grill.

Photograph opposite (bottom)

Gourmet Tip
If you do not have an ice cream or sorbet maker, Vanilla Parfait (pages 12-13) may be used instead of vanilla ice cream. To serve, dust with icing sugar after browning, or pour Fruit Purée (page 8) over the ice cream.

Bilberry Ice Cream with Crème Fraîche

Serves 6
Preparation time: 20 mins plus freezing·
435 kcal/1820 kJ

600 g/1¼ lb blueberries or blackberries

150 ml/¼ pt/⅔ cup sugar syrup flavoured with vanilla (page 8)

45 ml/3 tbsp rum

juice of 1 lemon

500 ml/18 fl oz/2¼ cups crème fraîche

mint leaves

icing sugar to garnish

1 Wash the berries, reserving a handful for garnishing. Bring the vanilla sugar syrup to the boil with the remaining berries and pass the mixture through a sieve into a bowl; do not use the residue left in the sieve. Mix the fruit purée with the rum and lemon juice to taste, stand the bowl in a second bowl full of ice cubes and stir until cold. Freeze in an ice cream or sorbet maker.
2 Cut out balls of ice cream with a spoon and place on chilled plates. Beat the crème fraîche with the balloon whisk and pour over the ice cream. Garnish with a few berries, mint leaves and sugar.

Photograph opposite (top)

41

Elderberry Sorbet

Serves 6
Preparation time: 1¹/₂
hours plus freezing
240 kcal/1005 kJ

---

*350 g/12 oz elderberries,
taken off stalks*

*50 g/2 oz/¹/₄ cup caster
sugar*

*400 ml/14 fl oz/1³/₄ cups
Sugar Syrup (page 8)*

*150 ml/¹/₄ pt/²/₃ cup white
wine*

4 cloves

juice of 1 lemon

*20 ml/1¹/₂ tbsp elderberry
liqueur or home-made fruit
wine*

1 Put the elderberries into a pan, mix with the sugar and leave to draw for 1 hour. Place the sugar syrup, white wine and cloves in a second pan, bring to the boil and strain over the elderberries.

2 Heat the mixture and boil for 6 to 8 minutes, then purée very finely in a blender. Flavour to taste with the lemon juice and liqueur or wine and allow to cool. Freeze in an ice cream or sorbet maker.

3 Twist out balls of sorbet with a spoon and arrange on chilled oval plates.

Photograph (left)

Apple Sorbet

Serves 6
Preparation time: 45 mins
plus freezing
225 kcal/930 kJ

---

*400 ml/**14 fl oz**/1³/₄ cups*
Sugar Syrup (page 8)

*150 ml/¹/₄ **pt**/²/₃ cup white*
sparkling wine

*350 g/**12 oz** dessert apples*

juice of 1 lemon

*45 ml/**3 tbsp** Calvados*

a few mint leaves

a few raspberries or wild
strawberries

---

1 Put the sugar syrup and the wine in a pan and bring to the boil. Peel and quarter the apples, removing the cores. Add the pieces of apple and the lemon juice to the sugar syrup and wine. Bring to the boil and cook for 5 minutes. Work to a purée in a blender then push through a fine sieve using a wooden spoon. Stir in the Calvados. Allow the mixture to cool then freeze in an ice cream or sorbet maker.

2 Use a forcing bag with a star nozzle to pipe the sorbet into chilled champagne glasses; garnish with mint leaves and raspberries or wild strawberries.

Photograph (right)

Plum Sorbet

Serves 6
Preparation time: 45 mins
plus freezing
220 kcal/920 kJ

---

100 g/**4 oz**/³/₄ cup prunes

lukewarm water

225 g/**8 oz** dessert plums

300 ml/¹/₄ **pt**/1 ¹/₄ cups Sugar Syrup (page 8)

150 ml/¹/₄ **pt**/²/₃ cup fresh orange juice

150 ml/¹/₄ **pt**/²/₃ cup white wine

3 cloves

1 cinnamon stick

45 ml/**3 tbsp** Armagnac

juice of 1 lemon

---

1 Soak the prunes for 1 to 3 hours in lukewarm water, then remove the stones from both the prunes and the plums.
2 Put the sugar syrup, orange juice, wine, cloves and cinnamon stick into a pan and bring to the boil. Cook for 3 to 5 minutes, then strain through a fine sieve into the pan. Add the prunes and plums and boil for 3 minutes.
3 Purée the mixture very finely in a blender, pass through a sieve and flavour to taste with the Armagnac and lemon juice. Leave to cool. Freeze in an ice cream or sorbet maker.

Photograph opposite (top)

Granita of Vineyard Peaches

Serves 6
Preparation time: 1 ¹/₄ hours plus freezing
230 kcal/955 kJ

---

350 g/**12 oz** peaches

300 ml/¹/₂ **pt**/1 ¹/₄ cups white wine

juice of 1 lemon

200 ml/**7 fl oz**/scant 1 cup Sugar Syrup (page 8)

1 vanilla pod

1 quantity Raspberry Purée (page 8)

20 ml/1 ¹/₂ **tbsp** raspberry liqueur

12 raspberries

lime leaves

---

1 Scald the peaches and remove the skins. Halve the fruit, but do not remove the stones. Place the wine, lemon juice, sugar syrup and vanilla pod in a pan and poach the half-peaches in the liquid for about 10 minutes or until soft.
2 Remove the vanilla pod, stone the peaches and pass the fruit flesh and liquid through a sieve.
3 Put the mixture in a shallow dish and place in the freezer. Stir well several times until frozen.
4 Prepare the raspberry purée and mix with the liqueur. Place the granita in chilled dishes; garnish with the raspberry purée, raspberries and the lime leaves.

Photograph opposite (bottom left)

Cherry Granita

Serves 6
Preparation time: 1 hour plus freezing
290 kcal/1215 kJ

---

350 g/**12 oz** Morello cherries

300 ml/¹/₂ **pt**/1 ¹/₄ cups red wine

200 ml/**7 fl oz**/scant 1 cup Sugar Syrup (page 8)

1 stick cinnamon

juice of 1 orange

20 ml/1 ¹/₂ **tbsp** cherry liqueur

300 ml/¹/₂ **pt**/1 ¹/₄ cups whipping cream, lightly whipped

5 ml/**1 tsp** cinnamon

---

1 Stone the cherries. Bring the stones to the boil with the red wine, sugar syrup, cinnamon stick and orange juice. Strain. Put the cherries into the liquid, bring to the boil and bubble for 3 to 5 minutes. Purée the mixture in a blender and pass through a fine sieve. Flavour to taste with the cherry liqueur and stir the mixture well. Place in the freezer and stir frequently until ice crystals form.
2 Arrange the granita in chilled dishes; garnish with the lightly whipped cream and the powdered cinnamon.

Photograph opposite (bottom right)

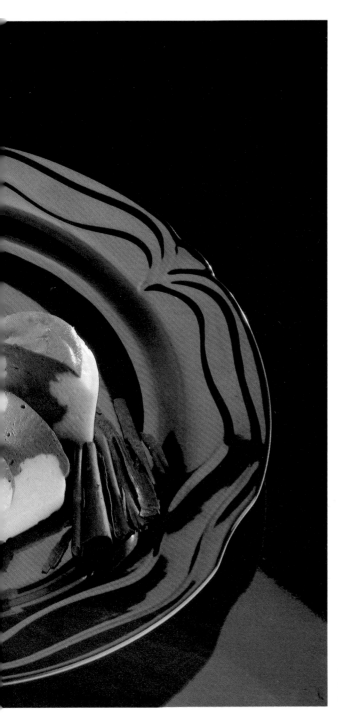

Light Surprises – Creams, Whips and Mousses

These delicate creams and frothy creations are a part of the standard repertoire of haute cuisine and are often simpler to make than they look. Moreover, these air-filled desserts can always provide pleasurable surprises because there are so many unusual combinations.

Orange-Chocolate Cream with Strawberry Purée, page 48

Orange-Chocolate Cream with Strawberry Purée

Serves 6
Preparation time: 1¼ hours plus chilling and garnishing
470 kcal/1995 kJ plus garnish

---

5 egg yolks

150 g/5 oz/⅓ cup caster sugar

150 ml/¼ pt/⅔ cup white wine

300 ml/½ pt/1¼ cups fresh orange juice

25 ml/5 tsp gelatine

30 ml/2 tbsp cold water

45 ml/3 tbsp orange liqueur

400 ml/14 fl oz/1¾ cups whipping cream, whipped

60 g/2½ oz cooking chocolate

chocolate flakes

1 quantity Strawberry Purée (page 8) or 1 quantity Coffee Liqueur Zabaglione (page 59)

---

1 Place the egg yolks in a pan with the sugar and mix briefly. Heat the wine and the orange juice in a second pan, strain off and fold carefully into the egg yolk mixture. Heat gently, stirring continuously, and beat until the mixture is thick enough to coat the back of a spoon.

2 Soften the gelatine in the cold water, pour into a saucepan and melt gently over a low heat. Add the liqueur, then stir into the egg mixture.

3 Place the pan in a bowl containing ice cubes and stir the cream until cold. Fold the whipped cream into the mixture. Rinse 6 moulds or a dish with cold water and allow to drain. Fill with half the cream.

4 Put the cooking chocolate into a bowl and dissolve over hot water. Stir the cooled but still liquid chocolate into the second half of the cream. Using a forcing bag with a star nozzle, squeeze the chocolate cream into the semi-solid orange cream. Chill in the refrigerator for 2 to 3 hours.

5 Turn the cream out carefully on to the plates and garnish with flakes of chocolate. Pour the strawberry purée or coffee liqueur zabaglione on to the plate.

Photograph page 46

Vanilla Cream

Serves 6
Preparation time: 2 hours
360 kcal/1495 kJ

---

pulp from 1 vanilla pod

150 ml/¼ pt/⅔ cup milk

75 g/3 oz/1/3 cup caster sugar

3 eggs, separated

40 g/1½ oz chocolate

1 quantity each of Pear, Kiwi and Raspberry Purées (page 8)

a few lemon balm leaves

---

1 Put the vanilla pulp into a pan with the milk and bring to the boil. Strain. Put one third of the caster sugar into a bowl with the egg yolks and add the strained milk.

2 Beat over a pan of hot water until the mixture is thick. Place the bowl in a larger one containing ice cubes and continue beating until the mixture is cold.

3 Whisk the egg whites, add the remaining caster sugar and continue whisking until the mixture is very stiff. Fold the egg whites carefully into the vanilla mixture.

4 Make the fourth garnish (page 15) from the bar of chocolate and fruit purées. Place the vanilla cream next to the garnish in spoonfuls and garnish with a few leaves of lemon balm.

Photograph opposite

49

Curd Cheese Cream

Serves 6
Preparation time: 45 mins
plus chilling
200 kcal/845 kJ

---

3 eggs, separated

*150 g/**5 oz**/²/₃ cup caster sugar*

*225 g/**8 oz** curd cheese*

grated rind of 1 orange

fruit as desired

icing sugar to garnish

---

1 Place the egg yolks and half the sugar in a bowl and heat until thick over hot water, beating all the time. Stand bowl in a second bowl of ice cubes and stir the mixture until cold. Squeeze out the curd cheese in a cloth so that it is dry. Add the curd cheese and the orange rind to the egg yolk mixture and beat well until the mixture is frothy and creamy. Chill for at least 30 minutes in the refrigerator.
2 Whisk the egg whites slowly, gradually adding the remaining caster sugar, and continue whisking the whole mixture until light and stiff. Fold into the curd cheese mixture.
3 Use a forcing bag with a star nozzle to pipe the curd cream into deep flameproof bowls. Brown quickly under a hot grill then decorate with fruit and icing sugar.

Photograph (top)

Yoghurt Cream with Apricots

Serves 6
Preparation time: 1½ hours plus chilling
740 kcal/3085 kJ

---

*450 ml/³/₄ **pt**/2 cups natural yoghurt*

---

*60 g/2½ **oz**/¹/₄ cup caster sugar*

---

*20 ml/1½ **tbsp** apricot jam*

---

1 envelope gelatine

---

*30 ml/**2 tbsp** warm water*

---

*20 ml/1½ **tbsp** apricot brandy*

---

*400 ml/**14 fl oz**/4³/₄ cups whipping cream, whipped*

---

juice and grated rind of ¹/₂ lemon

---

1 quantity Custard Sauce (page 9)

---

1 quantity Chocolate Sauce (page 9)

---

a few lemon balm leaves

---

1 Mix the yoghurt, sugar and apricot jam; pass the mixture through a sieve. Soften the gelatine in water, and add it to the apricot brandy.

2 Reserve a few tablespoons of the cream. Fold the remainder into the yoghurt with lemon juice and rind. Pour into moulds, chill for 3 hours.

3 Garnish the chilled plates with custard and chocolate sauces as shown in the sixth garnish (page 15). Turn out the moulds and garnish with the leaves and reserved cream.

Photograph (bottom)

Prune Curd Cheese Cream

Serves 6
Preparation time: 1 hour plus soaking
345 kcal/1450 kJ

175 g/6 oz stoned prunes

45 ml/3 tbsp port

60 ml/4 tbsp orange juice

60 ml/4 tbsp milk

1 envelope gelatine

15 ml/1 tbsp cold water

100 g/4 oz curd cheese

2 egg yolks

5 ml/1 tsp grated orange rind

4 egg whites

60 g/2½ oz/¼ cup caster sugar

300 ml/½ pt/²/₃ cup whipping cream, whipped

45 ml/3 tbsp cognac

1 Soak the prunes in the port and orange juice for 2 to 3 hours. Remove the stones and purée the prunes and juices in a blender. Bring the purée to the boil with the milk. Soften the gelatine in a pan with the water and melt over a low heat. Stir into the prune mixture.
2 Pass the curd cheese through a sieve and beat with the egg yolks until frothy. Stir into the purée with the orange rind.
3 Beat the egg whites until thick. Gradually add the sugar and continue to beat until the mixture is stiff. Lightly fold into the prune and curd cheese mixture with the cream

and cognac. Spoon into moulds and refrigerate until set.

Photograph opposite (top)

Goat's Cheese with Strawberry Purée

Serves 6
Preparation time: 1 hour
320 kcal/1335 kJ

350 g/12 oz goat's cheese

30 ml/2 tbsp soured cream

100 g/4 oz grated apple

a little lemon juice

20 ml/1½ tbsp Calvados

salt

1 quantity Strawberry Purée (page 8)

10 ml/2 tsp green peppercorns

a few strawberries

1 Pass the goat's cheese through a sieve and beat with the soured cream until smooth. Mix the grated apple with the lemon juice and Calvados. Fold into the cheese mixture and salt lightly.
2 Prepare the strawberry purée and mix with the peppercorns in a bowl.
3 Pour the strawberry purée on to chilled plates. Cut out balls of cheese mixture with a spoon and arrange as desired on the strawberry purée. Garnish with strawberries.

Photograph opposite (bottom left)

Cream Cheese with Lemon and Blueberries

Serves 6
Preparation time: 40 mins plus chilling
345 kcal/1435 kJ

225 g/8 oz cream cheese

2 egg yolks

75 g/3 oz/¹/₃ cup caster sugar

juice of 1 lemon

25 g/1 oz/2 tbsp vanilla sugar

60 ml/4 tbsp whipping cream, whipped

150 ml/¹/₄ pt/²/₃ cup Sugar Syrup (page 8)

20 ml/1½ tbsp rum

350 g/12 oz blueberries

1 Put the cream cheese, egg yolks, caster sugar, lemon juice and vanilla sugar into a bowl and beat until frothy. Fold in the whipped cream.
2 Bring the sugar syrup to the boil, add the rum and the blueberries, bring back to the boil and boil briefly for 2 or 3 minutes. Leave to cool.
3 Fill a forcing bag with the cream cheese mixture and, using a star nozzle, pipe rings or rosettes on a porcelain or glass plate. Surround with the cooked blueberries.

Photograph opposite (bottom right)

Stilton Cream with Walnuts and Fruit

Serves 6
Preparation time: 1$^1/_4$ hours plus soaking
400 kcal/1655 kJ

Cream:

---

*225 g/**8 oz** Stilton cheese*

---

*100 g/**4 oz**/$^1/_2$ cup butter, softened*

---

*200 ml/1 $^1/_2$ **tbsp** pear liqueur*

Fruit Salad:

---

36 large grapes

---

*225 g/**8 oz** pears*

---

2 kiwi fruits

---

*60 ml/**4 tbsp** Sugar Syrup (page 8)*

---

juice of $^1/_2$ lemon

---

*20 ml/1 $^1/_2$ **tbsp** honey*

---

*20 ml/1 $^1/_2$ **tbsp** pear liqueur*

---

18 walnut halves

---

1 Pass the Stilton through a sieve then beat in the butter with the pear liqueur. Beat the mixture until light and creamy.
2 Peel the grapes, removing the pips with the point of a knife. Peel and quarter the pears and remove the cores. Cut into 24 slices. Peel the kiwi fruits and cut into 12 slices. Pour the sugar syrup, lemon juice, honey and pear liqueur into a bowl and mix well. Transfer the fruit to a bowl and coat with the syrup. Leave to draw for 1 hour.

3 Arrange the fruit on flat plates as desired. Put the cheese mixture into a forcing bag with a star nozzle, pipe into the centre of the plate and garnish with the walnuts.

Gourmet Tip
If Stilton cheese is unavailable, use French Roquefort or Danish Blue.

Black and White Chocolate Terrine

Serves 6
Preparation time: 1³/₄ hours plus chilling
850 kcal/3555 kJ

Light Mixture:

100 g/*4 oz* white chocolate

2 egg whites

60 g/*2¹/₂ oz*/*¹/₄ cup* caster sugar

150 ml/*¹/₄ pt*/*²/₃ cup* double cream, whipped

a few drops of almond essence

Dark Mixture:

100 g/*4 oz* plain chocolate

2 egg whites

60 g/*2¹/₂ oz*/*¹/₄ cup* caster sugar

150 ml/*¹/₄ pt*/*²/₃ cup* double cream, whipped

Sauce:

500 ml/*18 fl oz*/*2¹/₄ cups* milk

50 g/*1¹/₂ oz* filter coffee powder

10 ml/*2 tsp* cocoa powder

60 g/*2¹/₂ oz*/*¹/₄ cup* caster sugar

75 g/*3 oz* plain chocolate

10 ml/*2 tsp* gelatine

20 ml/*1¹/₂ tbsp* coffee liqueur

25 g/*1 oz*/2 tbsp butter, melted

60 ml/*4 tbsp* cream

2 egg yolks

150 ml/*¹/₄ pt*/*²/₃ cup* whipping cream

a few mint leaves

1 To make the light-coloured mixture, put the white chocolate in a bowl and melt over hot water. Whip the egg whites until thick, gradually beat in sugar and continue beating until mixture is stiff. Fold in the melted chocolate with the cream and almond essence.
2 Combine the ingredients for the dark mixture in the same way but omit the almond essence.
3 Moisten a loaf tin and line with clingfilm (see page 12). Firstly, pour in the white mixture diagonally (tip the mould sideways to do this). Place in the refrigerator at this angle until it has set. Turn the mould upright, pour in the dark chocolate mixture and return to the refrigerator. Chill a further 2 to 3 hours.
4 To make the sauce, bring the milk to the boil with the coffee powder, pass through a paper filter and return to the pan. Add the cocoa, sugar and chocolate. Bring to the boil, stirring continuously. Soften the gelatine in the liqueur, pour into a saucepan and melt over a low heat. Carefully stir into the chocolate mixture with the melted butter. Whisk the cream with the egg yolks then fold smoothly into the sauce. Leave to cool. Stir the sauce thoroughly from time to time to prevent a skin forming.
5 Whip the whipping cream until semi-stiff. Use the fifth garnish (page 15) for decoration. Remove the terrine from the mould, slice it and garnish with mint leaves.

Photograph opposite

Gourmet Tip
When cutting the terrine, it is a good idea to dip the knife in hot water after cutting each slice. This way no traces of cream are left on the knife and the cut surface is smooth.

Blood Orange Zabaglione

Serves 6
Preparation time: 30 mins
115 kcal/485 kJ

*150 ml/¹/₄ **pt**/²/₃ cup white wine*
juice of 1 lemon
*300 ml/¹/₂ **pt**/1¹/₄ cups blood orange juice*
*40 g/1¹/₂ **oz**/3 tbsp caster sugar*
4 egg yolks
grated rind of 1 lemon
*20 ml/1¹/₂ **tbsp** Cointreau*

1 Pour the wine, lemon juice, blood orange juice, sugar and egg yolks into a bowl and whisk over hot water until the mixture is foamy and thick. Flavour to taste with the grated orange rind and the Cointreau, and beat again.
2 Pour into large glass goblets and serve warm.

Photograph (left)

58

Coffee Liqueur Zabaglione

Serves 6
Preparation time: 30 mins
120 kcal/510 kJ

---

*25 g/**1 oz** Turkish filter coffee powder*

---

*300 ml/¹/₂ **pt**/²/₃ cup cold water*

---

4 egg yolks

---

*60 g/**2¹/₂ oz**/¹/₄ cup caster sugar*

---

*75 ml/**5 tbsp** coffee liqueur*

filter coffee powder to garnish

---

1 Boil the coffee powder with the water, allow it to bubble up 3 times, then clear it with a dessert-spoonful of cold water. Pour through a paper filter and measure. If there is more than 150 ml/¹/₄ pt/²/₃ cup, the liquid must be boiled down to concentrate it; if there is less, add a little water to make up the quantity.
2 Beat the egg yolks and sugar until thick, stir in the hot coffee carefully, then continue to beat over hot water until the mixture is thick and frothy. Flavour to taste with the coffee liqueur and beat again.
3 Pour into large glass goblets, sprinkle with the coffee powder and serve whilst still warm.

Photograph (right)

Raspberry Whip

Serves 6
Preparation time: 1½ hours plus chilling
470 kcal/1965 kJ

---

225 g/**8 oz** raspberries

175 g/**6 oz**/³/₄ cup caster sugar

1 envelope gelatine

30 ml/**2 tbsp** cold water

20 ml/**1½ tbsp** raspberry liqueur

300 ml/**½ pt**/1¼ cups whipping cream, whipped

4 egg whites

1 quantity Custard Sauce (page 9)

1 quantity Raspberry Purée (page 8)

a few raspberries

---

1 Pass the raspberries through a sieve and mix with half the sugar. Soften the gelatine in the cold water, pour into a saucepan and melt over a low heat. Add to raspberries with liqueur.
2 Place the bowl containing the raspberries in iced water; stir until the mixture thickens. Fold in the cream. Whip the egg whites until stiff, stir in the remaining sugar lightly and fold into the raspberry mixture. Pour into 6 moulds and chill in the refrigerator for 2 to 3 hours or until set.
3 Garnish chilled plates with custard sauce and fruit purée as the sixth garnish (page 15). Dip the moulds quickly in hot water, turn out on to plates and decorate with the whole raspberries.

Photograph opposite (top)

Almond Whip with Nougat

Serves 6
Preparation time: 1¼ hours plus chilling
500 kcal/2085 kJ

---

200 g/**7 oz** bar chocolate with praline filling

5 eggs, separated

60 ml/**4 tbsp** Sugar Syrup (page 8)

45 ml/**3 tbsp** Amaretto

300 ml/**½ pt**/1¼ cups double cream

40 g/**1½ oz**/3 tbsp caster sugar

30 ml/**2 tbsp** flaked almonds, lightly browned

---

1 Break up the chocolate and melt it in a bowl resting over a pan of hot water. Put the egg yolks in a second bowl with the sugar syrup and beat over hot water until the mixture is warm, thick and creamy. Flavour to taste with the Amaretto and stir into the chocolate mixture. Allow to cool slightly.
2 Whip half the cream. Beat the egg whites until thick. Gradually beat in the sugar until the mixture is very stiff.
3 Gently stir the cream into the chocolate mixture while it is still warm. Fold in the beaten egg whites and sugar with a metal spoon.
4 When smooth and well-combined, pour the almond whip into 6 glass bowls, cover with clingfilm and chill well in the refrigerator.
5 Whip the remaining cream and pipe on to the almond whip. Decorate with flaked almonds.

Photograph opposite (bottom)

White Chocolate Mousse

Serves 6
Preparation time: 1¹/₄ hours plus chilling
815 kcal/3400 kJ

---

300 ml/¹/₂ pt/1¹/₄ cups single cream

300 g/11 oz white chocolate

60 g/2¹/₂ oz/¹/₄ cup butter, cut into flakes and at room temperature

1 envelope gelatine

30 ml/2 tbsp cold water

2 eggs

20 ml/1¹/₂ tbsp Crème de Cacao

500 ml/18 fl oz/2¹/₄ cups whipping cream, whipped

grated rind and segments of 6 tangerines

20 ml/1¹/₂ tbsp tangerine liqueur

a few lime leaves

chocolate flakes

1 Bring the cream to the boil. Break up the chocolate. Remove the pan of cream from the heat and add the chocolate. Place the pan in a bowl of hot water and allow the chocolate to melt. Stir in the butter. Soften the gelatine in cold water, pour into a pan and melt over a low heat. Mix into the hot chocolate mixture.

2 Mix the egg yolks with the cocoa liqueur in a bowl. Fold in the chocolate mixture smoothly. Allow to cool. Reserve a little whipped cream for garnish and fold in the remaining cream, stiffly beaten egg whites and tangerine rind. Chill for 2 to 3 hours.

3 Separate the tangerine segments from their skins and sprinkle with tangerine liqueur.

4 Arrange the tangerine segments on chilled plates. Dip a spoon in hot water and cut out balls of the mousse. Depending on the size of the spoon, place 3 or 4 balls on the plate and garnish with the remainder of the whipped cream, lime leaves and flaked chocolate.

Index of Recipes

Foulsham
Yeovil Road, Slough, Berkshire, SL1 4JH
ISBN 0-572-01660-3
This English language edition copyright
© 1991 W. Foulsham & Co. Ltd.
Originally published by Falken-Verlag,
GmbH, Niedernhausen TS, West
Germany.
Photographs copyright © Falken Verlag.

Printed in Portugal